COMPOSER SHOWCASE

HAL LEONARD
STUDENT PIANO LIBRARY

Au Chocolat

ORIGINAL PIANO SOLOS IN IMPRESSIONIST STYLE

BY JENNIFER LINN

I dedicate this collection to the love of my life,
Mark Linn, whom I adore even more than chocolate.

ISBN 978-1-5400-5754-9

HAL•LEONARD®

Copyright © 2019 by HAL LEONARD LLC
International Copyright Secured   All Rights Reserved

Visit Hal Leonard Online at
www.halleonard.com

Contact us:
Hal Leonard
7777 West Bluemound Road
Milwaukee, WI 53213
Email: info@halleonard.com

In Europe, contact:
Hal Leonard Europe Limited
42 Wigmore Street
Marylebone, London, W1U 2RN
Email: info@halleonardeurope.com

In Australia, contact:
Hal Leonard Australia Pty. Ltd.
4 Lentara Court
Cheltenham, Victoria, 3192 Australia
Email: info@halleonard.com.au

GLOSSARY OF FRENCH TERMS

FRENCH	TRANSLATION	FRENCH	TRANSLATION
accéléré	accelerate	*joyeux*	happy, cheerful
animant	lively, brisk	*la fin*	the end
animé	animated	*laisser vibrer*	let ring
beignets	donuts	*macarons*	light merinque-based cookies
au chocolat	chocolate	*mélanger doucement*	gently blend
au revoir	goodbye	*mousse*	foamy, frothy dessert
avec amour	with love	*Nöel*	Christmas
avec un ami	with a friend	*neige soudaine*	sudden snow
bonne journée	good day	*opéra*	opera
bûche	log	*premier*	first
cédez	yield, relax tempo	*ralentir*	slow down
chanter doucement	sing sweetly	*retenu*	holding back
en chantant	singing	*sans pédale*	without pedal
crémeux	creamy	*saveur riche*	rich flavor
derrière le rideau	behind the curtain	*savourer*	savor
doux	soft, sweet	*soufflé*	puffy egg-based dessert
éclair	oblong cream-filled pastries	*toucher soyeux*	silky touch
frénétique	frantic, frenzied	*tranquille*	quiet, peaceful
gâteau	cake	*un peu*	a little
hésitant	hesitant		

CONTENTS

Beignets au chocolat
Chocolate Donuts

Jennifer Linn

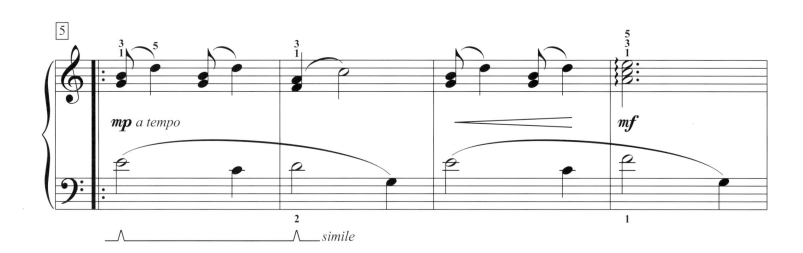

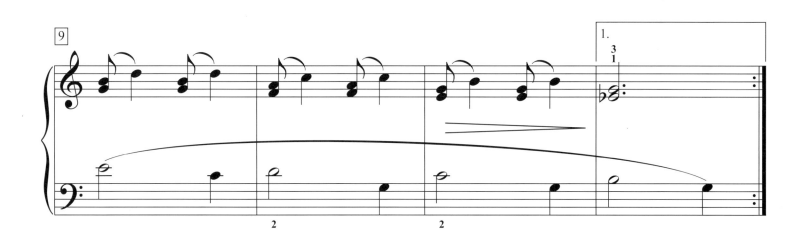

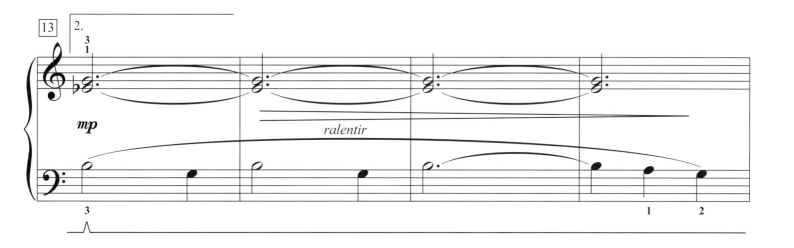

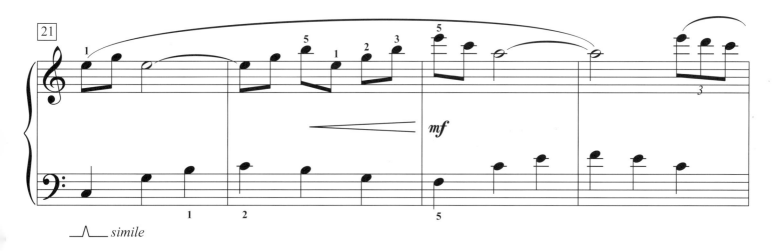

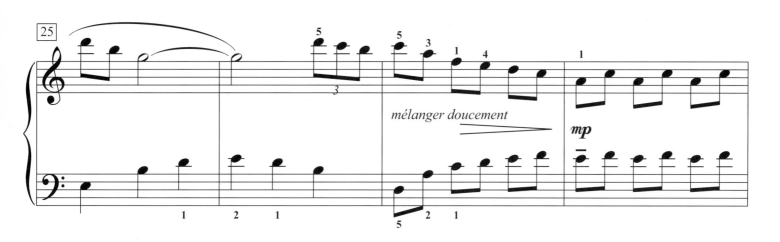

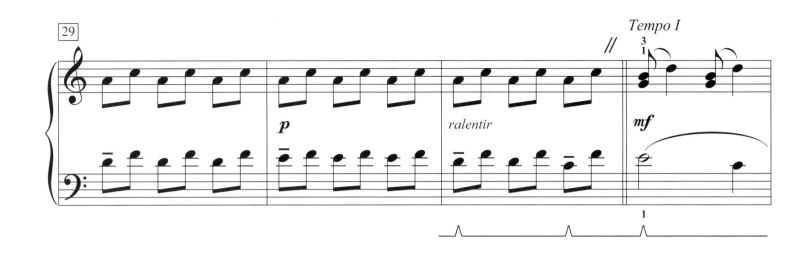

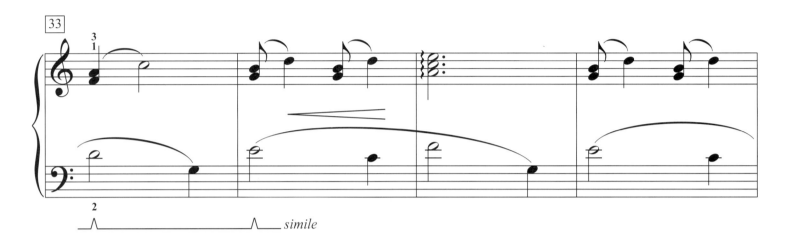

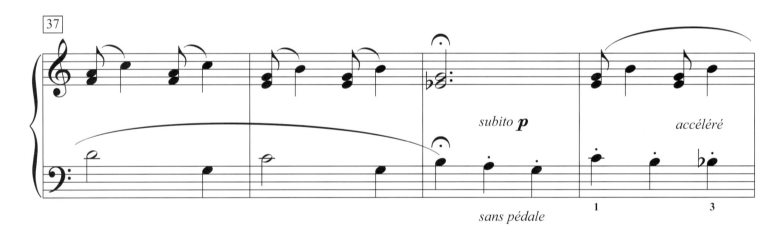

Soufflé au chocolat

Chocolate Souffle

Jennifer Linn

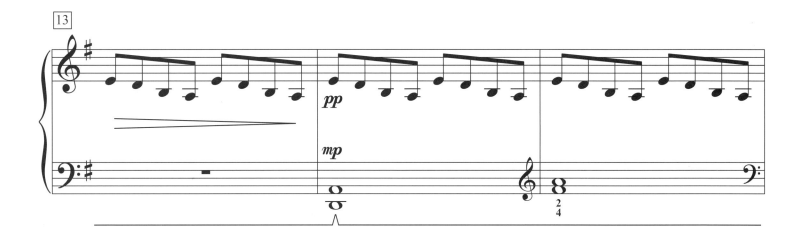

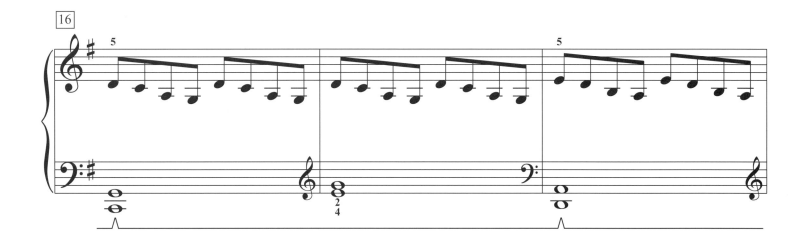

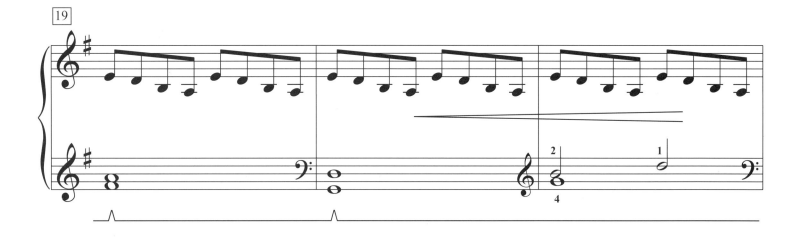

Macarons au chocolat

Chocolate Macarons

Jennifer Linn

Mousse au chocolat
Chocolate Mousse

Jennifer Linn

Frénétique (♩ = 160-172)

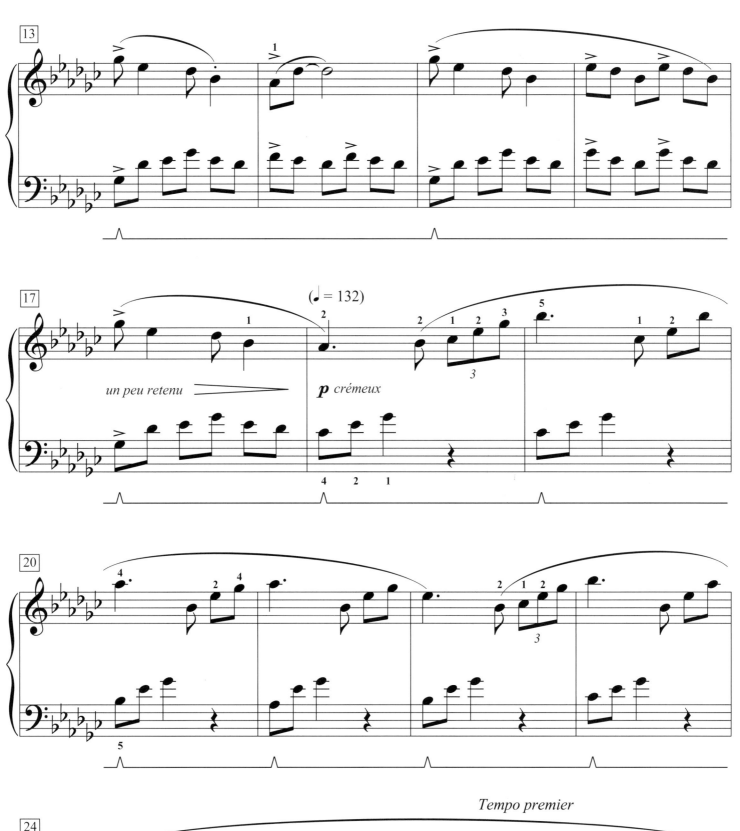

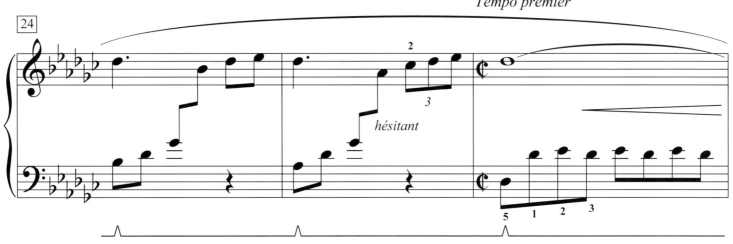

Éclair au chocolat
Chocolate Eclair

Jennifer Linn

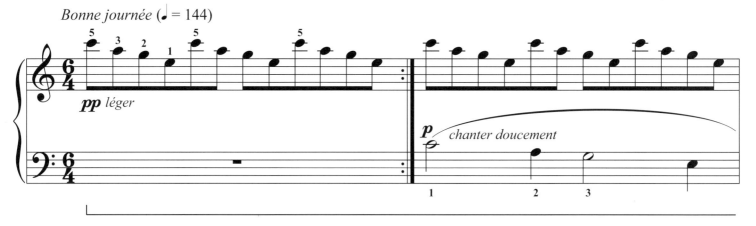

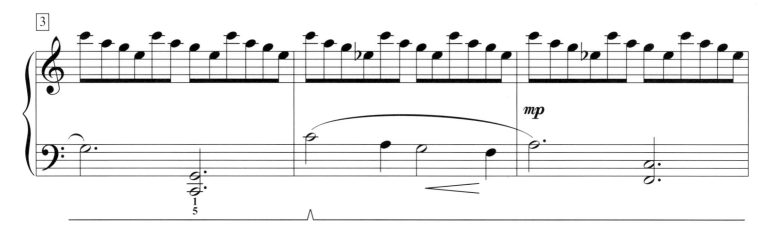

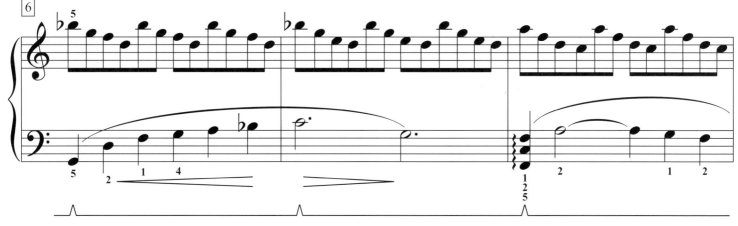

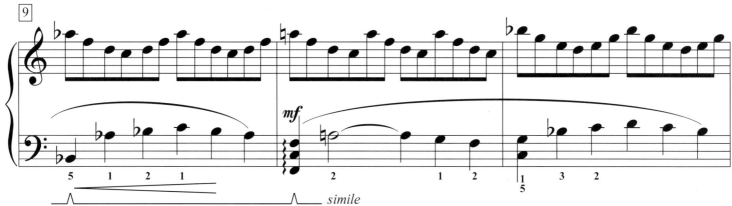

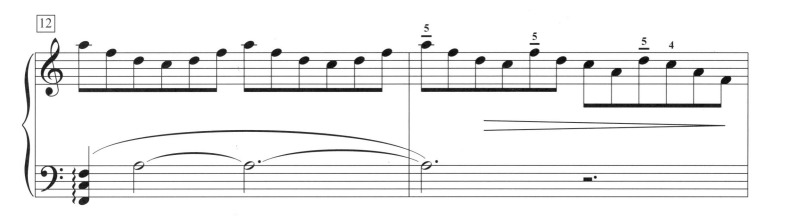

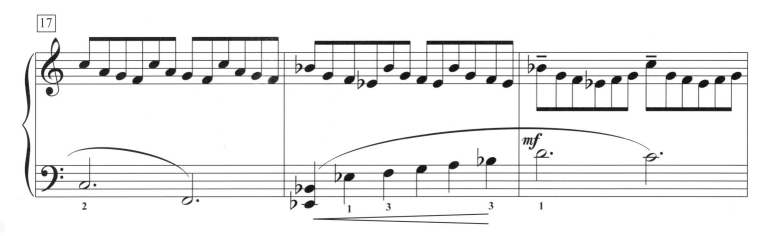

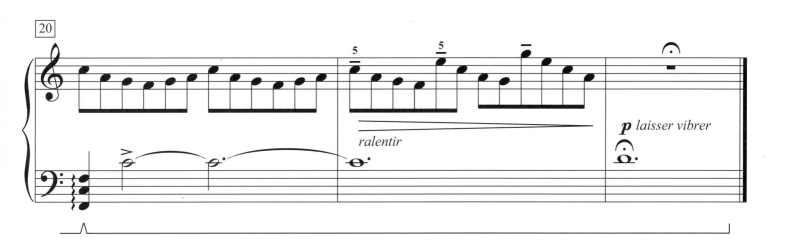

Gâteau d'Opéra
Opera Cake

Jennifer Linn

Bûche de Noël
Yule Log Cake

Jennifer Linn

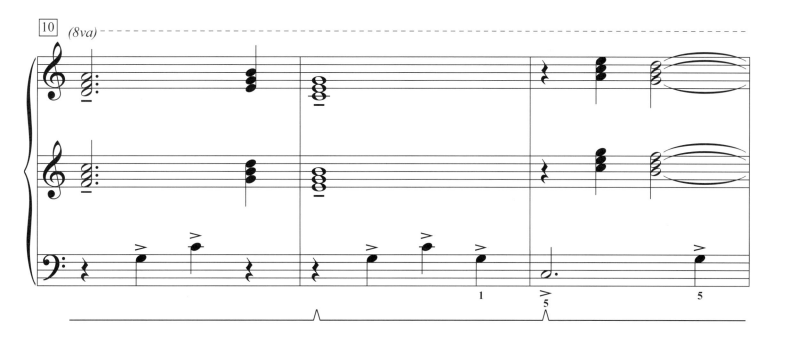

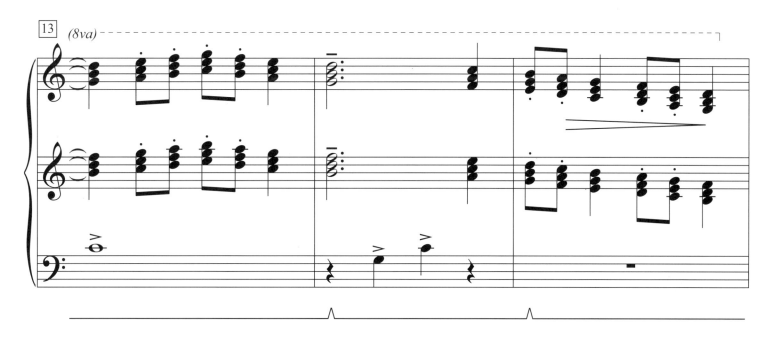

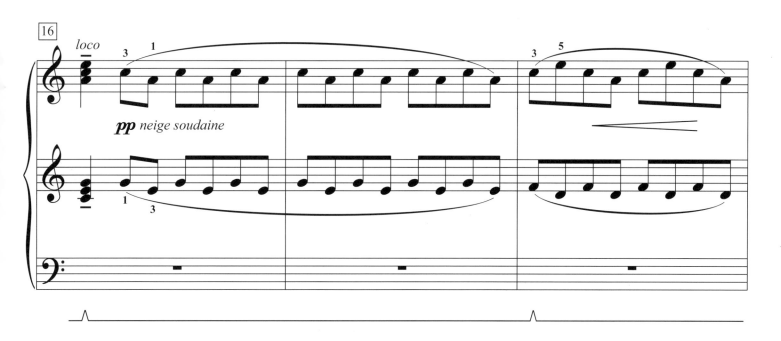

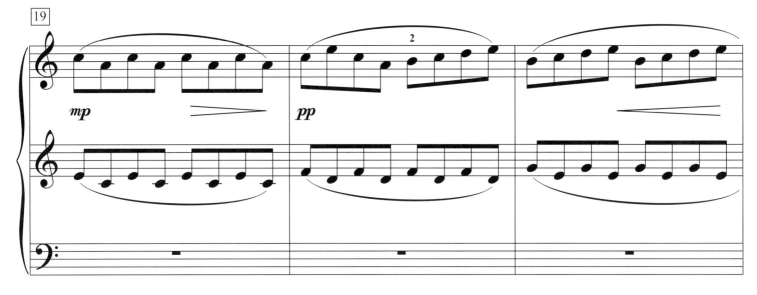

_⌃_ simile

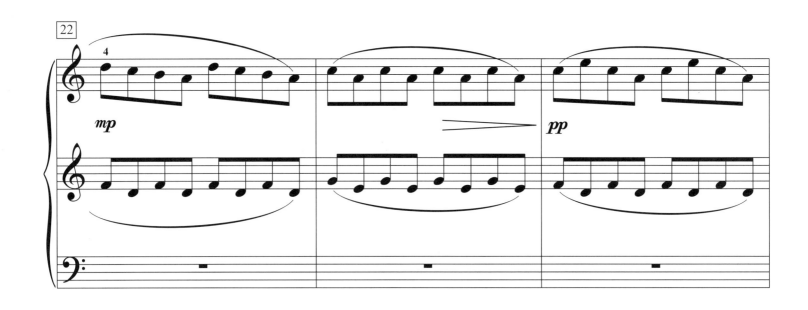

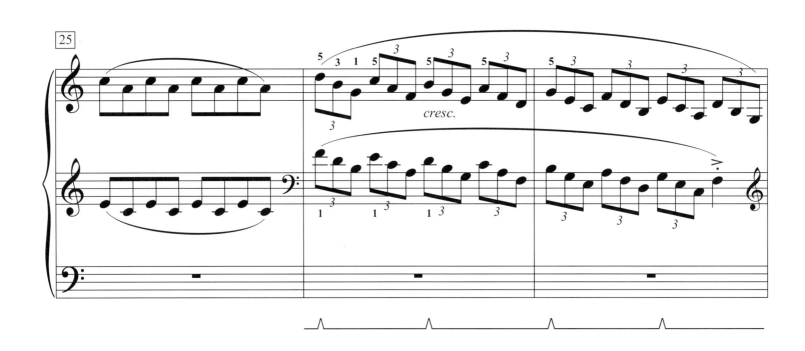

This series showcases great original piano music from our **Hal Leonard Student Piano Library** family of composers. Carefully graded for easy selection.

COMPOSER SHOWCASE
HAL LEONARD STUDENT PIANO LIBRARY®

BILL BOYD

JAZZ BITS (AND PIECES)
Early Intermediate Level
00290312 11 Solos................................$7.99

JAZZ DELIGHTS
Intermediate Level
00240435 11 Solos................................$8.99

JAZZ FEST
Intermediate Level
00240436 10 Solos................................$8.99

JAZZ PRELIMS
Early Elementary Level
00290032 12 Solos................................$7.99

JAZZ SKETCHES
Intermediate Level
00220001 8 Solos..................................$8.99

JAZZ STARTERS
Elementary Level
00290425 10 Solos................................$7.99

JAZZ STARTERS II
Late Elementary Level
00290434 11 Solos................................$7.99

JAZZ STARTERS III
Late Elementary Level
00290465 12 Solos................................$8.99

THINK JAZZ!
Early Intermediate Level
00290417 Method Book..................$12.99

TONY CARAMIA

JAZZ MOODS
Intermediate Level
00296728 8 Solos..................................$6.95

SUITE DREAMS
Intermediate Level
00296775 4 Solos..................................$6.99

SONDRA CLARK

THREE ODD METERS
Intermediate Level
00296472 3 Duets................................$6.95

MATTHEW EDWARDS

CONCERTO FOR YOUNG PIANISTS
FOR 2 PIANOS, FOUR HANDS
Intermediate Level Book/CD
00296356 3 Movements $19.99

CONCERTO NO. 2 IN G MAJOR
FOR 2 PIANOS, 4 HANDS
Intermediate Level Book/CD
00296670 3 Movements...................$17.99

PHILLIP KEVEREN

MOUSE ON A MIRROR
Late Elementary Level
00296361 5 Solos..................................$8.99

MUSICAL MOODS
Elementary/Late Elementary Level
00296714 7 Solos..................................$6.99

SHIFTY-EYED BLUES
Late Elementary Level
00296374 5 Solos..................................$7.99

CAROL KLOSE

THE BEST OF CAROL KLOSE
Early Intermediate to Late Intermediate Level
00146151 15 Solos..............................$12.99

CORAL REEF SUITE
Late Elementary Level
00296354 7 Solos..................................$7.50

DESERT SUITE
Intermediate Level
00296667 6 Solos..................................$7.99

FANCIFUL WALTZES
Early Intermediate Level
00296473 5 Solos..................................$7.95

GARDEN TREASURES
Late Intermediate Level
00296787 5 Solos..................................$8.50

ROMANTIC EXPRESSIONS
Intermediate/Late Intermediate Level
00296923 5 Solos..................................$8.99

WATERCOLOR MINIATURES
Early Intermediate Level
00296848 7 Solos..................................$7.99

JENNIFER LINN

AMERICAN IMPRESSIONS
Intermediate Level
00296471 6 Solos..................................$8.99

ANIMALS HAVE FEELINGS TOO
Early Elementary/Elementary Level
00147789 8 Solos..................................$8.99

CHRISTMAS IMPRESSIONS
Intermediate Level
00296706 8 Solos..................................$8.99

JUST PINK
Elementary Level
00296722 9 Solos..................................$8.99

LES PETITES IMAGES
Late Elementary Level
00296664 7 Solos..................................$8.99

LES PETITES IMPRESSIONS
Intermediate Level
00296355 6 Solos..................................$7.99

REFLECTIONS
Late Intermediate Level
00296843 5 Solos..................................$8.99

TALES OF MYSTERY
Intermediate Level
00296769 6 Solos..................................$8.99

LYNDA LYBECK-ROBINSON

ALASKA SKETCHES
Early Intermediate Level
00119637 8 Solos..................................$7.99

AN AWESOME ADVENTURE
Late Elementary Level
00137563 ....$7.99

FOR THE BIRDS
Early Intermediate/Intermediate Level
00237078 ....$8.99

WHISPERING WOODS
Late Elementary Level
00275905 9 Solos..................................$8.99

MONA REJINO

CIRCUS SUITE
Late Elementary Level
00296665 5 Solos..................................$6.99

COLOR WHEEL
Early Intermediate Level
00201951 6 Solos..................................$8.99

JUST FOR KIDS
Elementary Level
00296840 8 Solos..................................$7.99

MERRY CHRISTMAS MEDLEYS
Intermediate Level
00296799 5 Solos..................................$8.99

MINIATURES IN STYLE
Intermediate Level
00148088 6 Solos..................................$8.99

PORTRAITS IN STYLE
Early Intermediate Level
00296507 6 Solos..................................$8.99

EUGÉNIE ROCHEROLLE

CELEBRATION SUITE
Intermediate Level
00152724 3 Duets (1 Piano, 4 Hands)..............$8.99

**ENCANTOS ESPAÑOLES
(SPANISH DELIGHTS)**
Intermediate Level
00125451 6 Solos..................................$8.99

JAMBALAYA
Intermediate Level
00296654 Ensemble (2 Pianos, 8 Hands).........$12.99

JAMBALAYA
Intermediate Level
00296725 Piano Duo (2 Pianos) $7.95

LITTLE BLUES CONCERTO
FOR 2 PIANOS, 4 HANDS
Early Intermediate Level
00142801 Piano Duo (2 Pianos, 4 Hands)........$12.99

TOUR FOR TWO
Late Elementary Level
00296832 6 Duets................................$7.99

TREASURES
Late Elementary/Early Intermediate Level
00296924 7 Solos..................................$8.99

JEREMY SISKIND

BIG APPLE JAZZ
Intermediate Level
00278209 8 Solos..................................$8.99

MYTHS AND MONSTERS
Late Elementary/Early Intermediate Level
00148148 9 Solos..................................$7.99

CHRISTOS TSITSAROS

DANCES FROM AROUND THE WORLD
Early Intermediate Level
00296688 7 Solos..................................$8.99

LYRIC BALLADS
Intermediate/Late Intermediate Level
00102404 6 Solos..................................$8.99

POETIC MOMENTS
Intermediate Level
00296403 8 Solos..................................$8.99

SEA DIARY
Early Intermediate Level
00253486 9 Solos..................................$8.99

SONATINA HUMORESQUE
Late Intermediate Level
00296772 3 Movements $6.99

SONGS WITHOUT WORDS
Intermediate Level
00296506 9 Solos..................................$9.99

THREE PRELUDES
Early Advanced Level
00130747 ....$8.99

THROUGHOUT THE YEAR
Late Elementary Level
00296723 12 Duets..............................$6.95

ADDITIONAL COLLECTIONS

AT THE LAKE
by Elvina Pearce
Elementary/Late Elementary Level
00131642 10 Solos and Duets.........................$7.99

COUNTY RAGTIME FESTIVAL
by Fred Kern
Intermediate Level
00296882 7 Rags..................................$7.99

LITTLE JAZZERS
by Jennifer Watts
Elementary/Late Elementary Level
00154573 Solos....................................8.99

PLAY THE BLUES!
by Luann Carman (Method Book)
Early Intermediate Level
00296357 10 Solos..............................$9.99

Prices, contents, and availability subject
to change without notice.

HAL•LEONARD®
www.halleonard.com